# Men

### by Ann Lindsay Mitchell

Lang**Syne**

**PUBLISHING**

WRITING *to* REMEMBER

Lang**Syne**

PUBLISHING

WRITING *to* REMEMBER

Vineyard Business Centre,
Pathhead, Midlothian EH37 5XP
Tel: 01875 321 203 Fax: 01875 321 233
E-mail: info@lang-syne.co.uk
www.langsyneshop.co.uk

Design by Dorothy Meikle
Printed by Ricoh Print Scotland
© Lang Syne Publishers Ltd 2011

ISBN 978-1-85217-079-0

# Menzies

**SEPT NAMES INCLUDE:**
Dewar
Macminn
Macmonies
Means
Mein
Minn
Minnus

# Menzies

**MOTTO:**
Will God I Shall.

**CLAN BADGE:**
Menzies Heath.

**TERRITORY:**
Atholl and Strathtay.

*Chapter one:*

# The origins of the clan system

by Rennie McOwan

**The original Scottish clans of the Highlands and the great families of the Lowlands and Borders were gatherings of families, relatives, allies and neighbours for mutual protection against rivals or invaders.**

Scotland experienced invasion from the Vikings, the Romans and English armies from the south. The Norman invasion of what is now England also had an influence on land-holding in Scotland. Some of these invaders stayed on and in time became 'Scottish'.

The word clan derives from the Gaelic language term 'clann', meaning children, and it was first used many centuries ago as communities were formed around tribal lands in glens and mountain fastnesses.

The format of clans changed over the centuries, but at its best the chief and his family held the land on behalf of all, like trustees, and the ordinary clansmen and women believed they had a blood relationship with the founder of their clan.

There were two way duties and obligations. An inadequate chief could be deposed and replaced by someone of greater ability.

Clan people had an immense pride in race. Their relationship with the chief was like adult children to a father and they had a real dignity.

The concept of clanship is very old and a more feudal notion of authority gradually crept in.

Pictland, for instance, was divided into seven principalities ruled by feudal leaders who were the strongest and most charismatic leaders of their particular groups.

By the sixth century the 'British' kingdoms of Strathclyde, Lothian and Celtic Dalriada (Argyll) had emerged and Scotland, as one nation, began to take shape in the time of King Kenneth MacAlpin.

Some chiefs claimed descent from

ancient kings which may not have been accurate in every case.

By the twelfth and thirteenth centuries the clans and families were more strongly brought under the central control of Scottish monarchs.

Lands were awarded and administered more and more under royal favour, yet the power of the area clan chiefs was still very great.

The long wars to ensure Scotland's independence against the expansionist ideas of English monarchs extended the influence of some clans and reduced the lands of others.

Those who supported Scotland's greatest king, Robert the Bruce, were awarded the territories of the families who had opposed his claim to the Scottish throne.

In the Scottish Borders country - the notorious Debatable Lands - the great families built up a ferocious reputation for providing warlike men accustomed to raiding into England and occasionally fighting one another.

Chiefs had the power to dispense justice

and to confiscate lands and clan warfare produced a society where martial virtues - courage, hardiness, tenacity - were greatly admired.

Gradually the relationship between the clans and the Crown became strained as Scottish monarchs became more orientated to life in the Lowlands and, on occasion, towards England.

The Highland clans spoke a different language, Gaelic, whereas the language of Lowland Scotland and the court was Scots and in more modern times, English.

Highlanders dressed differently, had different customs, and their wild mountain land sometimes seemed almost foreign to people living in the Lowlands.

It must be emphasised that Gaelic culture was very rich and story-telling, poetry, piping, the clarsach (harp) and other music all flourished and were greatly respected.

Highland culture was different from other parts of Scotland but it was not inferior or less sophisticated.

Central Government, whether in London

*"The spirit of the clan means much to
thousands of people"*

or Edinburgh, sometimes saw the Gaelic clans as a challenge to their authority and some sent expeditions into the Highlands and west to crush the power of the Lords of the Isles.

Nevertheless, when the eighteenth century Jacobite Risings came along the cause of the Stuarts was mainly supported by Highland clans.

The word Jacobite comes from the Latin for James - Jacobus. The Jacobites wanted to restore the exiled Stuarts to the throne of Britain.

The monarchies of Scotland and England became one in 1603 when King James VI of Scotland (1st of England) gained the English throne after Queen Elizabeth died.

The Union of Parliaments of Scotland and England, the Treaty of Union, took place in 1707.

Some Highland clans, of course, and Lowland families opposed the Jacobites and supported the incoming Hanoverians.

After the Jacobite cause finally went down at Culloden in 1746 a kind of ethnic cleansing took place. The power of the chiefs was curtailed. Tartan and the pipes were banned in law.

Many emigrated, some because they wanted to, some because they were evicted by force. In addition, many Highlanders left for the cities of the south to seek work.

Many of the clan lands became home to sheep and deer shooting estates.

But the warlike traditions of the clans and the great Lowland and Border families lived on, with their descendants fighting bravely for freedom in two world wars.

Remember the men from whence you came, says the Gaelic proverb, and to that could be added the role of many heroic women.

The spirit of the clan, of having roots, whether Highland or Lowland, means much to thousands of people.

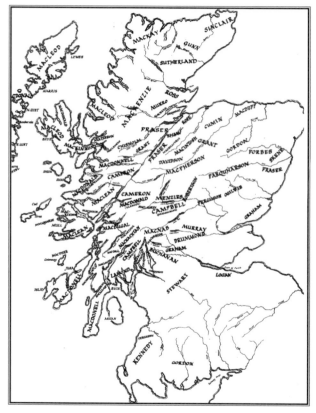

*A map of the clans' homelands*

*Chapter two:*

# What's in a name?

**The Menzies name poses a pronouncement puzzle for most people.**

Scots folk say 'Mingies', while others, and the spelling suggests this, say 'Menzies' exactly as it is written.

The reason for the first, correct pronunciation is due to the origins of the name, which is of almost certain French extraction.

The Menzies name and clan derives from the same English family of Manners of Etal, the head of which is the Duke of Rutland. Sir Iain Moncrieffe of that ilk, who was an expert on the genealogy of Scots families, explained that the name Menzies comes from the area of Mesnieres, near to Rouen in Normandy, and the reason the 'z' is never pronounced is because it is the old Scottish letter for guttural 'y', which is a cross between a 'y' and a 'g'.

Sir Iain had in his possession a charter

confirming the lands of Culdares in Glenlyon in western Perthshire. These lands were given to the first Menzies family to appear in the Scottish records "as freely, quietly, fully and honourable as any baron within the Kingdom of Scotland is able to give to any such land". In this early thirteenth century document the granter (whose seal shows a shield Barry of six) calls himself Robert de Meyneris and also Thomas de Meyneris.

The first Menzies chief was present at the court of Alexander II by 1224 and became Chamberlain of Scotland by 1249. In common with so many other acquisitions of lands and goods and chattels in those days, things were frequently not as straightforward as they might at first appear, and there was much secret shuffling of favours. Sir Robert acquired a large amount of land in Rannoch, an area which could well have been part of the abbey lands of Dull near Aberfeldy.

Dull receives its curious name due to St Adamnan, a disciple of St Columba, who spent his working life in Glenlyon, where he was remembered best for saving the lives of his followers from the plague. He climbed up on a rock then known as Craig-diannaidh, the 'rock of safety', exhorted the plague to enter a hole within the rock, and sent his people sensibly up into the hills of Glenlyon, where they escaped the disease. When he died, he asked for his body to be carried down the glen, and where the first tie or 'dull' on his coffin chafed and broke, he was to be buried there. The first tie broke at Tulli, and there, as he requested, he was buried. But at Tulli there already existed a place of learning, a church and sanctuary at which Adamnan had preached regularly. So a more fitting place would have been hard to find and the name was changed from Tulli to Dull.

Dull is a mile at the most from the present Castle Menzies, and the story demonstrates that the area was a place of established ecclesiastical history, and considerable importance.

Also in the area were relics which demonstrated the robust and populated history of the area. There is a church dedicated to St Ciaran and

Clach-na-Cruich, or Stone of the Measles. It has
on the upper side a cavity which contained rain
water, and it was this water which, when drunk by
the patient, was reputed to cure the illness. People
would flock from miles away to drink from its
cups, of which there were seven, a number which
added to its mystic reputation. Not for nothing
was it Christened the 'Menzies Charm stone'.

The county was also famous for its Celtic
towers or forts, as well as mote hills, cairns and
cists. In the middle of the 19 century, a circular urn
was discovered with zig zag patterns.

Thus this granting of these lands was a
singular honour. So why did the King grant Sir
Robert Menzies such a prize?

The answer possibly lies in a favour. Two
of Sir Robert's sons were given the very royal
names of Alexander and David, names which
were rarely given to those not of royal birth. This
points to their mother, Sir Robert's wife, being of
royal descent. It appears that as she is not recorded as one of King Alexander's legitimate children,
that it seems very likely she was an illegitimate

lady of royal birth. She must have been someone of considerable importance, hence the granting of her in marriage, and the impressive gift of lands which accompanied her.

Just down the road at Strathtay from Dull, the stronghold of the Menzies chief was his fortified residence known as 'Meinnearch' in Gaelic, and was situated near Weem. In 1510, Sir Robert Menzies of that Ilk, the then chief resigned his baronies of Ennoch (possibly Rannoch) and Weem into the hands of James IV who granted them to him as the free barony of Menzies, renaming his castle as Castle Menzies.

This charter records an earlier charter, when his residence at Weem was destroyed by malefactors, described by his descendant Sir Iain Moncrieffe as 'ferocious whelps descended from the Wolf of Badenoch', a legendary character by the name of Stewart who even in the fearsome battlegrounds of clan warfare in the Middle Ages was head and shoulders in stature and dastardly deeds above his contemporaries.

These destroyers of the Menzies strong-

hold were the Stewarts of Garth, which is just at
the entrance to Glenlyon from Strathtay. The
items lost were listed in the Privy Council Decree
against Neil Stewart of Fortingall and include a
great deal of armour, four cannon and substantial
furnishings.

*Chapter three:*

# Sacrifice and loyalty

**By the sixteenth century, the Menzies chiefs were having regular skirmishes with their neighbouring landowners. The Campbells of Glenorchy were edging the Menzies lands, and trying to take more areas by force.**

Perhaps due to the sheer size and desolation of their western lands, the great acres of Rannoch Moor and the fact that their lands had no natural boundaries, like a sea coastline, others too were constantly harrying their land.

The Macdonnells of Keppoch, known as Clan Rannoch of Lochaber seized and fortified the island on Loch Rannoch against Menzies control, but an especially virulent and energetic raiding clan were evocatively known as the 'Children of the Mist'. They were a branch of the Clan Gregor, who had no lands in their own right, and were therefore always on the lookout for areas to purloin; more daring than the others, as they had nothing of their own to lose.

So with such threatening neighbours surrounding their lands and constantly reminding the
Menzies of their presence, the new Menzies
stronghold needed to be well fortified. James
Menzies of that Ilk built a castle to serve such
needs. He also served as a baron in the parliament
of Mary, Queen of Scots.

Castle Menzies stands today in a largely
unaltered form to when it was built in 1577.

Built on the fashionabl 'z' plan of its day,
with gun emplacements situated to cover both the
front and back doors, it has stood the test of time,
and its survival owes much to the strength of its
building as well as a concerted effort by the Clan
Menzies Society who rescued and restored it from
a ruin last century.

Ironically, the only time it was put to use
and tested as a stronghold was not by the Menzies
Chiefs themselves, but when it was used as a gar-
rison by the Hanoverian troops during the 1745
Jacobite Rising.

The Menzies were naturally on the side of

the Jacobites in the Risings, and on the 4th April, 1716, one of the Menzies chieftains, Alexander Menzies, was put on trial in Southwark, London for rebellion and high treason. Menzies 'pled the King's Pardon in regard of his extraordinary case, and those who drew him into the rebellion being about to possess his estate'. This was a direct reference to the Earl of Breadalbane, who was believed to have acted as a double agent, supporting the Jacobite cause for his own ends.

He was supposed to have given the Hanoverians information about the Menzies support for the Jacobites, Breadalbane hoping that his information would induce the Government to reward his support by gifting him the confiscated Menzies lands.

But while Menzies was aware of this, he was restrained in his condemnation. In a letter sent to his wife he comments that the Duke of Argyle arrived in London to plead for the cause of some imprisoned Atholl men. "He will be sparing for the Athole men's lives; I will not answer for their purses" – an oblique reference to the bribing abilities of the Duke, and his readiness, in Menzies eyes, to bend the law.

He later informed his wife that "the mob here has altered (their allegiance) since we came here, that there is no going out to our trials for them. My Lord Darenwater's brother and I were in our coach yesterday to our trials, but the mob stopped the coach and notwithstanding that our coach had six soldiers, they had almost drawn us out. All the ladies in the mob cried and wept and cried that the Almighty would preserve us against all our enemies. When we than went in our coach to Westminster, the coach I was in was a long way behind the rest, but we almost never could come back, twenty thousand followed us".

But despite the feelings of the crowd, Menzies was sentenced to death. In a neat turn of events, it was the Duke of Argyll who managed to secure a reprieve.

Another Menzies, this time Chieftain Archibald of Culdares was also awaiting trial for treason. His two sons had been captured earlier and flung into the dungeons of Carlisle Castle, but owing to the reputation of the family were released after a few months. They both immediately travelled to London to see if they could visit their father, by then waiting for his day of execution. Both the sons, Archibald and James, were fair haired, and they dressed themselves up as women and were admitted to the prison, whereupon one of them suggested that his father should swap clothes with him and effect an escape, leaving the son behind. But Archibald senior refused, pointing out that the son he left behind would "after the lenity shown them by the Government, it would be ungrateful to engage in such an affair and might be productive of unpleasant consequences…".

The sons then left their father, sure that this would be the very last time they would be able to see him alive.

However, he was very soon released, on the grounds that this story of his refusing to escape was a self sacrificing and noble act, and given a full pardon. He died in 1776.

By the time Bonnie Prince Charlie

appeared in the area in the next uprising in 1745, the Menzies were setting examples of a different kind. The Prince spent several days between Blair Castle and Menzies Castle. Lady Menzies provided elaborate hospitality for the Prince with ten courses set for him and eight courses for his aide de camp. The entire party, consisting of seventy in the Prince's retinue alone, dined in splendour in the Banqueting Hall at the Castle.

As the Prince travelled around the Highlands, other Highland ladies, the Countess of Perth and Lady MacIntosh, vied with each other to set a lavish table, following the precedent set by Lady Menzies.

She was to suffer greatly for her loyalty and generosity. When the Government troops reached the Castle, they unceremoniously flung out both her and her husband, who was lame, and both of them had to seek refuge up the glen.

Several years later, a third cousin of this chieftain, John Menzies, left for the West Indies to make his fortune. There does not seem to be a record of what he actually did there, but he was a successful businessman, and managed to make a considerable fortune. Indeed so busy was Sir John at amassing money that he rarely if ever wrote home. As the years rolled on, back home in Menzies Castle and the surrounding estate, Sir John was given up for dead. And so matters might have stood.

However, the then chieftain, Sir Robert, died without leaving any successors. A young descendant, also named Robert, was deemed to be the next in line, as his cousin John who would have been the inheritor seemed to have vanished years ago. Young Robert therefore took over the estates, as tradition dictated, free of debts and not affected by entail. This all took several months, and when at last all was accomplished, a grand ball and celebrations were planned. All day there were comings and goings, as the clansmen and tenants gathered from all around to join in the party. Bonfires were lit all over the Vale of Menzies and Castle Menzies, it was reported, was ablaze from top to bottom with candle light.

The ball commenced in the evening, with

the ladies dressed in gowns or sashes of the distinctive scarlet and white Menzies tartan.

At midnight a loud knocking was heard on the front door, and the servant, upon opening up the castle, was confronted by an exhausted figure, vaguely familiar in face, but very bronzed, standing beside a tired horse.

The servant had never seen this stranger before, and his clothing and appearance was so foreign to him that he quickly realised that this was not some latecomer to the ball, but a total stranger to the area.

The visitor asked if Sir Robert was at hand, and if so to give him the card he then proffered. The servant hastened up to the Banqueting Hall upstairs, signalled to Sir Robert to follow him out of the hall and handed him the card.

As Sir Robert gazed at the card, his face became ashen and he clutched the banister rail. Shaking, he descended the stairs, and there found his long lost cousin John.

John, no doubt taking in at a glance the situation, immediately clutched his cousin and reassured him not to put himself out. But Robert insisted that John should come in and take over the castle, his due inheritance, at once.

The two cousins argued quietly, but John who wished to give his cousin no distress, blankly refused to entertain Robert's offer of taking over the castle then and there and insisted that he would then take his leave, spend the night at the Weem Hotel, and Robert was to return to his guests.

But Robert and his wife retired after their guests had departed, not to sleep but to pack up their belongings. This they did during the night, telling no one what had happened, and when dawn broke, they left the castle for Edinburgh. But on the way they left a message at the Weem Hotel, congratulating John on his inheritance, and wishing him all possible happiness and health.

The reason for John's arrival was not purely down to chance. A Highland servant of his in the West Indies had always kept in touch with his family, and it was through one of those relatives that he had heard of the demise of old Sir

Robert, and knew that his master, John, was the nearest direct descendant. John had journeyed home to the astonishment of all his relatives. But not only did he make life as easy as he could for his ousted cousin, he also was wealthy enough to enhance the estate. Within a short time of taking over the estate, he married the beautiful daughter of the 4th duke of Atholl, the Honourable Charlotte Murray, whose portrait was hung in Castle Menzies.

The castle was around a century old when Colonel James, a brother of the chief of the time, SIr Alexander Menzies of that Ilk, was wounded in a skirmish with the Macdonalds of Glencoe. He suffered no less than nine arrow wounds in his thighs and legs.

*Chapter four:*

# Family fortunes

**Other Menzies sewed the seeds of their fame and fortune. A descendant of a Menzies of Culdares brought back the larch, now a vital tree in the forestation of Scotland, introducing this tree in 1737 from the Tyrol, where he gave the seed to the enthusiastic tree planting Duke of Atholl. He planted the first larch trees in the sanctuary grounds of the Cathedral of Dunkeld, on his lands, and one of these trees became the 'parent larch' of all the many hundreds of thousands of trees in Scotland.**

A further plant hunting Menzies was Archibald, born in 1754. He was of lowlier birth, brought up in Weem, and commenced his botanic life by working as a gardener in the Royal Botanic Gardens in Edinburgh.

Dr John Hope encouraged him to collect specimen plants in the Highlands. He was clearly a man of considerable aptitude, intelligence and adventure. He then trained in medicine, joined the Navy as an assistant surgeon and served in the American Wars of Independence.

Archibald took part in two round the world voyages, with Captain Corbett in 1786-89 and on the Discovery with Captain Vancouver in 1790-95. His major find was the monkey puzzle tree, or Chilean Pine, which graced many gardens in Scotland and further afield. He ended his career as a doctor in London, dying in 1842.

Precisely ten years later, another Menzies was born in Edinburgh who was to make his mark in Scotland, and whose legacy lives on today.

John Ross Menzies was the son of another John, who was born in 1808, and after schooling in his hometown went off to London to learn the bookselling trade, where he was apprenticed to the publisher Charles Tilt.

Returning to Edinburgh in 1833 he established himself rapidly as a small bookseller in Princes Street. This was in 1833, and John Menzies Senior had the advantage of his many contacts in London and by 1837 he was the agent to Chapman Hall, the publishers of 'The Pickwick Papers'. This was followed in 1841 with Punch magazine and the establishment of the wholesale side of the magazine business.

The retail and wholesale side of the book trade kept him fully employed and occupied into about 1855, when he extended his interests into wholesale newspaper distribution to newsagents. But a transformation was happening to transport in the United Kingdom, and John Menzies attached himself to this innovation rapidly. The train network was being established in the country and Menzies saw in this an excellent way in which to advance his business.

In 1857, the first John Menzies Bookstalls were opened at Perth, Stirling and Bridge of Allan. As the rail network spread, so did the bookstalls, and it was a rare railway halt which did not have an integral newsagent and bookshop on the station forecourt.

By now John Menzies had two young sons, and the elder of these, John Ross Menzies, born in 1852, along with his brother Charles were already in the business in 1867, when the name was changed to John Menzies and Co. By the turn of the century it was one of the top five book-selling companies in the UK.

As well as their many and varied achievements, the Menzies Clan have an added quirk when it comes to both the pronouncement of their name anf their tartan. The Menzies motto reveals such idiosyncrasies as 'Gael 'us Dearg a suas' or 'Up with the white and the red'. This refers to their distinctive scarlet and white tartan, claimed to be one of the oldest, as well as simplest recorded tartans.

The Hunting tartan, with the white check replaced in green is said to represent the mountain ash, or rowan tree, the plant emblem of the clan, and the black and white version is commonly known as the mourning Menzies cloth. A writer in 1892 recalled passing a shawl of this colouring on a washing line beside a cottage, hung there to show respect for the death of a Menzies Chieftain.